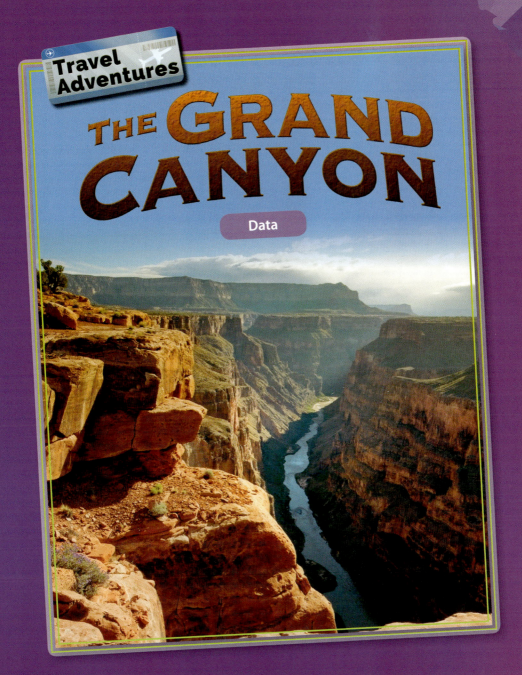

Consultants

Michele Ogden, Ed.D
Principal, Irvine Unified School District

Jennifer Robertson, M.A.Ed.
Teacher, Huntington Beach City School District

Publishing Credits
Rachelle Cracchiolo, M.S.Ed., *Publisher*
Conni Medina, M.A.Ed., *Managing Editor*
Dona Herweck Rice, *Series Developer*
Emily R. Smith, M.A.Ed., *Series Developer*
Diana Kenney, M.A.Ed., NBCT, *Content Director*
Stacy Monsman, M.A., *Editor*
Kevin Panter, *Graphic Designer*

Image Credits: pp. 6–7 Mel Melcon/Los Angeles Times via Getty Images; p. 18 (bottom right) Harry Taylor Dorling Kindersley Science Source; p. 20 (top, middle, bottom) Dorling Kindersley/Getty Images; p. 25 Didier Descouens Wikimedia Commons License: Creative Commons BY-SA 4.0 https://goo.gl/2GNGQ4; p. 27 LOC [LC-DIG-ppmsca-36042]; all other images from iStock and/or Shutterstock.

Teacher Created Materials
5301 Oceanus Drive
Huntington Beach, CA 92649-1030
http://www.tcmpub.com

ISBN 978-1-4807-5808-7
© 2018 Teacher Created Materials, Inc.
Made in China
Nordica.022017.CA21700227

Table of Contents

The Grand Canyon 4

The Journey Down 6

A Canyon Is Carved 10

Rock Stars, Rock Groups 14

Prehistoric Preserves 21

A Grand Trip 26

Problem Solving 28

Glossary 30

Index..31

Answer Key.. 32

The Grand Canyon

Imagine staring into a 6,000-foot (1,800-meter) canyon. It is a long way to the bottom. Luckily, those who want to explore Grand Canyon National Park are not limited to staring. There are many trails that wind from the top to the bottom. Some people make the trek on foot. Others go by mule. Either way, the long trip to the bottom offers many chances to learn.

And many people want to make that trip! Millions of people visit the Grand Canyon each year. They travel from around the world to see the stunning views. The rocks of the canyon are a mosaic of colors. There are shades of red, orange, and brown. And with just one look, people wonder many things. How did this form? What is it made of? And, of course, how long does it take to get to the bottom and back to the top?

Toroweap Point offers a majestic view of the Grand Canyon and Colorado River.

The sun rises on the colorful canyon.

LET'S EXPLORE MATH

This line graph represents the number of visitors that traveled to the Grand Canyon from 2005 to 2015.

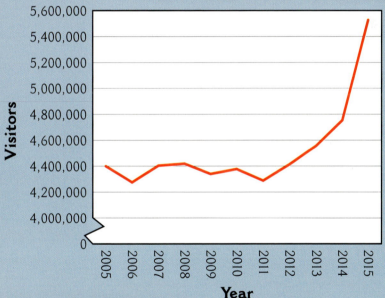

1. In which year did most people visit the Grand Canyon?

2. About how many more people traveled to the Grand Canyon in 2015 than in 2005?

3. About how many more visitors were there in 2014 than in 2006?

4. What is the scale used for the number of visitors?

The Journey Down

Visitors have a choice when they are ready to make that trip to the bottom of the canyon. For hikers, there are challenging trails. Trails made in the walls of the canyon curve, twist, and stretch all the way to the floor.

Other visitors saddle up! They enjoy a mule ride down to the bottom. Many parts of the trails are narrow and steep. But mules are surefooted animals. That means they have great balance. It is a safe, slow journey to the canyon floor. Riders travel in a mule train that is led by a **wrangler**. It takes many hours to reach the bottom by mule. So, riders spend the night there before heading back up to the top the next morning.

Visitors ride mules up the South Kaibab Trail.

LET'S EXPLORE MATH

These young mules have already made many trips to the bottom of the canyon. First, they travel down the Bright Angel Trail. On the way back up, they climb the South Kaibab Trail. See how many round-trip adventures Arrow, Joo Joo, Lottie, Owl, and Pups have made.

Mule	Round-Trips
Arrow	|||| ||||
Joo Joo	|||| ||||
Lottie	||||	
Owl	|||| ||
Pups	||||

1. How many more round-trips has Arrow made than Pups?
2. How many fewer round-trips has Lottie made than Owl?
3. How many round-trips have the mules made altogether?

A mule ride is a relaxing way to take in the Grand Canyon. But, there are also many trails for hiking. The Bright Angel Trail and the South Kaibab Trail are the two most common.

Hiking the trails on foot can be hard. But, it has its charm, too. Hikers can stop whenever they want. They can view the beauty of the canyon at their own pace. Or, visitors can join a guided hike. A ranger walks along with the hikers. The ranger can point out the natural features of the canyon.

Once at the bottom of the canyon, a hiker can rest or keep exploring. After all, there are new things to see. Or rather, there are old things that hikers are seeing for the first time! The Elves Chasm Gneiss (ELVES KAH-zum NICE) is the oldest rock in the canyon. It is part of the "basement" rocks because it sits below all other rocks.

LET'S EXPLORE MATH

This graph shows just a few of the many popular hiking trails at the Grand Canyon.

1. Which trail is the longest? About how many kilometers would the trail take round-trip? (Hint: The trail is the same length there and back.)

2. Which hike is longer, the hike to Coconino Saddle or to Horseshoe Mesa? How do you know?

3. Which two trails are shorter than the Grand View Trailhead to Horseshoe Mesa?

4. What is the scale used for the trail length?

A Canyon Is Carved

Journeys in the canyon begin and end at the top. From the top, some people say the Grand Canyon looks like a huge hole in the ground. Imagine the hole gets filled with dirt, sand, and rocks. Now, the top of it looks as flat as a pancake. This is what the region looked like when the Grand Canyon began to form. It was a huge stretch of flat land. And that land was made up of layer upon layer of rocks.

Scientists know that a powerful force had to cut through those layers of rock. That force was water. The Colorado River flowed down from the nearby mountains and crossed the flat land. The river then began to carve into the land. Millions of years passed. All the while, the mighty flow of the river kept cutting away the rock. And bit by bit, the canyon grew deeper.

The oldest rocks are at the bottom of the canyon.

A rugged rock pile makes an interesting formation on the South Kaibab Trail.

Snowmelt is another source of water in the canyon.

The Colorado River did not form the canyon by itself. Wind and rain cause rocks to wear down and break into small pieces. These pieces are called **sediment**. The wind and water move and carry it away. This process is called **erosion**.

A hiker who looks closely might notice cracks in the rocks. After a winter rain, water can freeze inside those cracks. Ice takes up more space than water. So, the cracks widen. The ice can even split the rocks. When it gets warmer, the ice melts back into water. This water carries away more sediment.

All of these forces work to change the canyon. So far, it has a depth of over 1 mile (1.8 km), a width of 11 mi. (18 km), and a length of 270 mi. (430 km). But the process continues. It keeps growing, little by little.

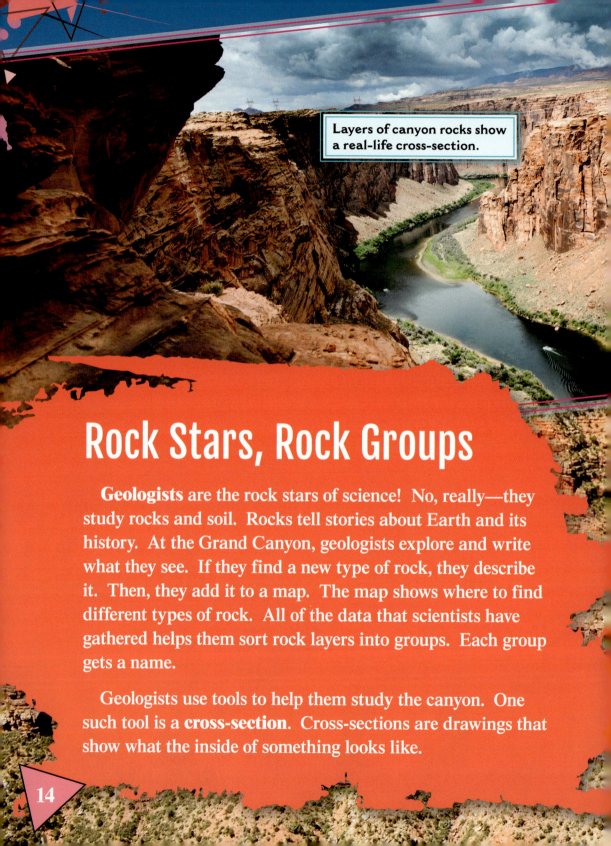

Layers of canyon rocks show a real-life cross-section.

Rock Stars, Rock Groups

Geologists are the rock stars of science! No, really—they study rocks and soil. Rocks tell stories about Earth and its history. At the Grand Canyon, geologists explore and write what they see. If they find a new type of rock, they describe it. Then, they add it to a map. The map shows where to find different types of rock. All of the data that scientists have gathered helps them sort rock layers into groups. Each group gets a name.

Geologists use tools to help them study the canyon. One such tool is a **cross-section**. Cross-sections are drawings that show what the inside of something looks like.

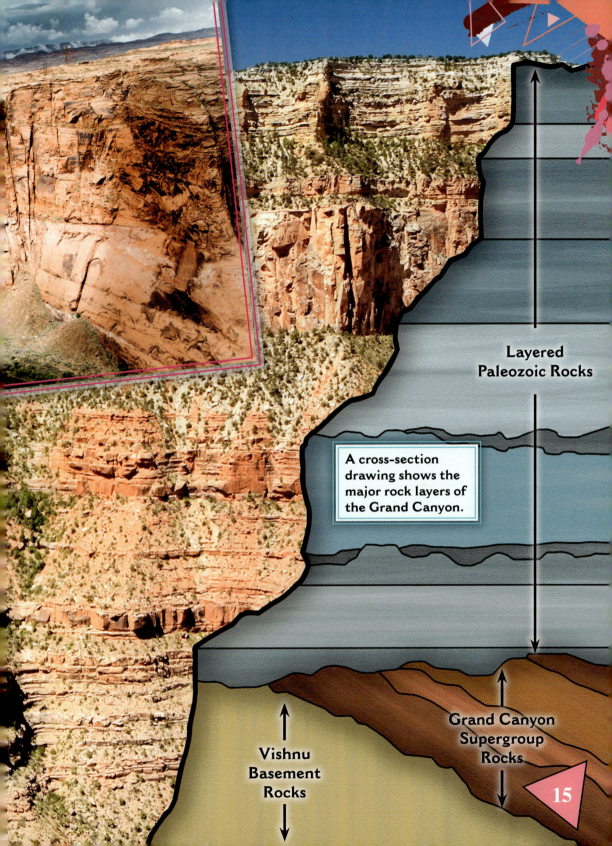

A cross-section drawing shows the major rock layers of the Grand Canyon.

Layered Paleozoic Rocks

Vishnu Basement Rocks

Grand Canyon Supergroup Rocks

15

Each layer of rock holds clues about the Grand Canyon's past. These clues track changes in the **environment** that happen over time. These small changes can add up. They result in big transformations. The spot where an ocean exists now may one day become a desert.

It took millions of years for these rock layers to form.

But do not plan on seeing an ocean dry up overnight! It is a slow process. It takes millions of years for a change like that to take place. When it does happen, the rocks that form will change, too. Imagine an ocean slowly drying out and becoming a desert. Then, desert rocks start to form. They form on top of the older ocean rocks. This is why so many types of rocks can be found in the Grand Canyon. The environment has changed many times over the years. New rocks have been placed on top of the older rocks each time.

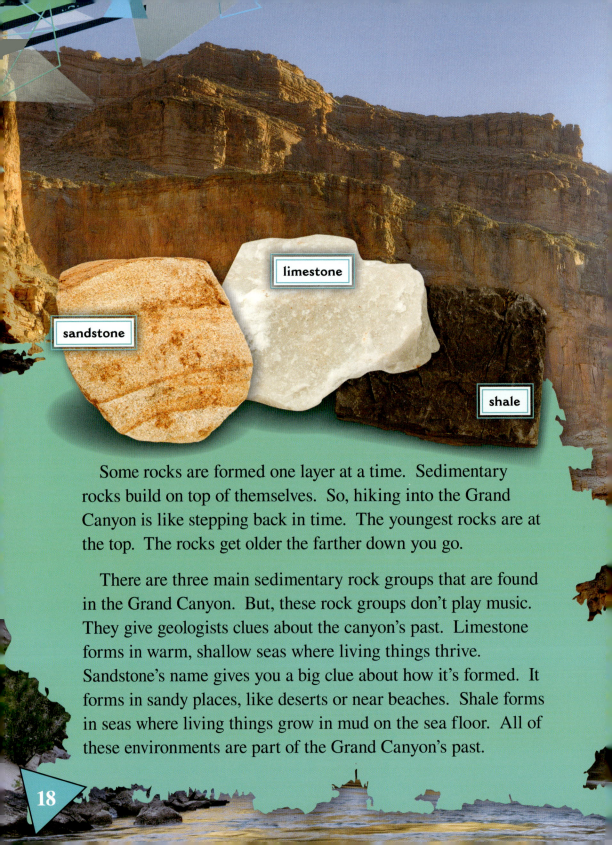

Some rocks are formed one layer at a time. Sedimentary rocks build on top of themselves. So, hiking into the Grand Canyon is like stepping back in time. The youngest rocks are at the top. The rocks get older the farther down you go.

There are three main sedimentary rock groups that are found in the Grand Canyon. But, these rock groups don't play music. They give geologists clues about the canyon's past. Limestone forms in warm, shallow seas where living things thrive. Sandstone's name gives you a big clue about how it's formed. It forms in sandy places, like deserts or near beaches. Shale forms in seas where living things grow in mud on the sea floor. All of these environments are part of the Grand Canyon's past.

LET'S EXPLORE MATH

Some rock layers of the Grand Canyon are thicker than others. This bar graph shows how thick some of those layers are.

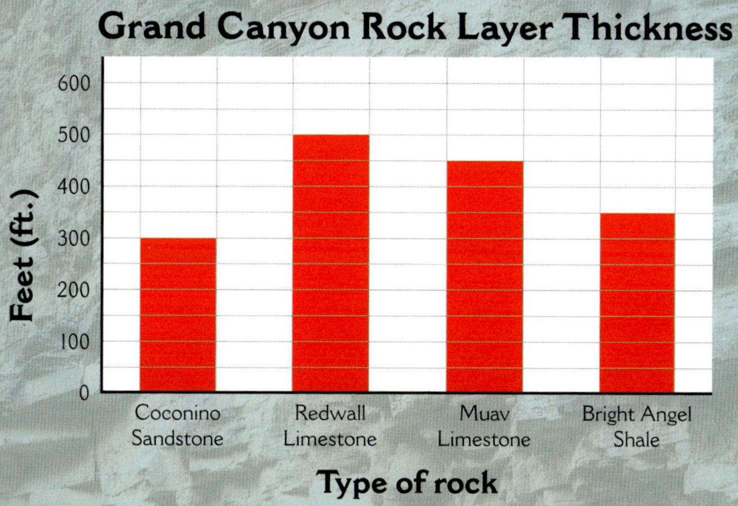

Grand Canyon Rock Layer Thickness

- Coconino Sandstone: 300 ft.
- Redwall Limestone: 500 ft.
- Muav Limestone: 450 ft.
- Bright Angel Shale: 350 ft.

1. Which type of rock has the thickest layer?
2. Which two layers of rocks have a layer thickness difference of 100 feet?
3. What is the difference, in feet, between the thickest and thinnest rock layers?

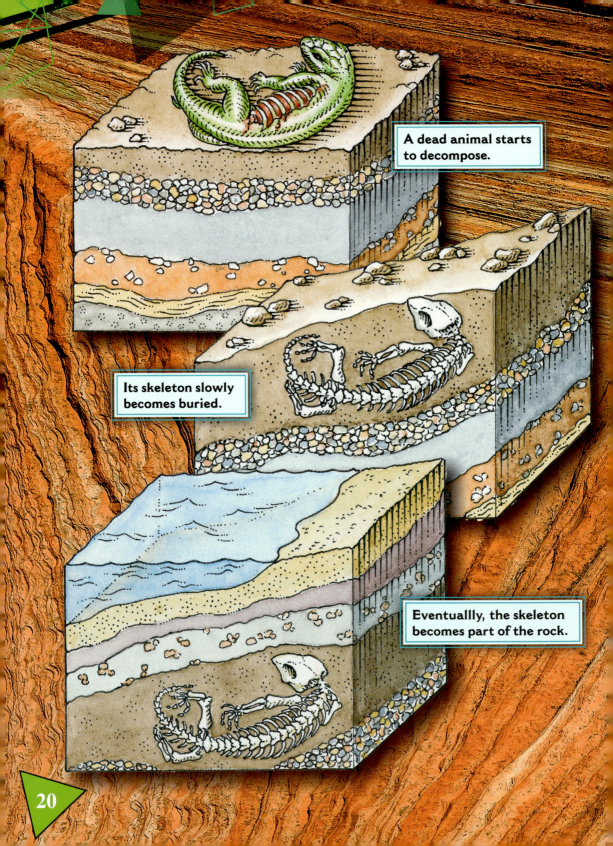

Prehistoric Preserves

Rocks made from sand and dust might not sound too special. After all, sedimentary rocks can be found everywhere. Plants live in them. Creatures build their homes in them, walk on them, and find food in them. But, these living things can also die in them. Sometimes, when a creature or plant dies, other living things eat it. Other times, sediment buries it. When this happens, a part of it gets **preserved**.

The soft parts of it will usually **decompose**. But the hard parts, like its bones and teeth, do not. So, the remains can be preserved. And as time goes on, the sediment will harden. It will slowly turn into rock. The hard parts of living things will become part of the rock, too. These are called **fossils**. In the Grand Canyon, very old animal tracks can be found in sandstone layers. Fossils of plants can be found in layers of shale. The rocks and their fossils tell more stories about the plant and animal life of the canyon.

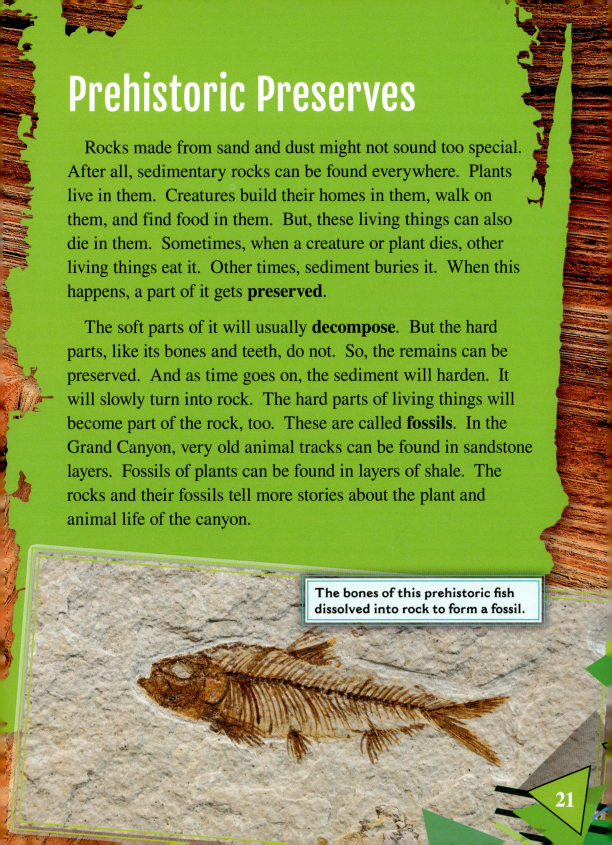

The bones of this prehistoric fish dissolved into rock to form a fossil.

Fossil Finds

The world is filled with millions of plant and animal **species**. Each thrives in certain places on Earth. And, as fossils, they can be found in the type of rock that formed where they died. With all of its layers of rocks, the Grand Canyon is packed with fossils.

Sea fossils are very common in the Grand Canyon. This is because sea environments formed many of the layers of rock. Extinct animals called *trilobites* (TRIGH-luh-bites) used to crawl around on the muddy sea floor. They had huge eyes. And they could roll into tight balls. Their fossils can be found in the sandstone, limestone, and shale layers of the Grand Canyon. There were other ancient sea animals, too. Horn corals did not crawl. Instead, they stuck to the soft sea floor. There, they waited for food to float by. Then, they used their tentacles to stun and grab prey. Horn coral fossils are found in limestone.

horn coral fossil

trilobite fossil

This is what a trilobite might have looked like millions of years ago.

23

Crinoid (KRY-noid) fossils can be found in the limestone layers of the Grand Canyon. They look like they are made of small, round discs that sit one on top of the other. The animals that formed these fossils had parts that anchored them to the sea floor. Those same parts also acted as feet. This helped them collect food and move from place to place.

Brachiopods (BRAY-kee-e-pads) are also found in the limestone layers. They lived on the sea floor, too. Each of these animals lived inside of two shells that could close tightly. They had strong muscles that helped their shells open and close.

crinoid fossil

Living crinoids look like this and still exist today.

During a family vacation, a group of cousins decide to have a fossil scavenger hunt along the South Kaibab Trail. They create a graph to show how many fossils of each kind they find. (Ranger Rules: They had to stay on the trail and leave the fossils where they found them.)

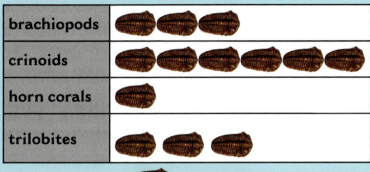

Fossil Scavenger Hunt

1. Which fossil did the cousins find the most of? How many did they find?

2. Which fossils did they find the same number of? How many of each did they find?

3. Which fossil did they find two times more of than the brachiopods?

brachiopod fossils

A Grand Trip

The Grand Canyon is so much more than just a huge hole in the ground. President Theodore Roosevelt once said it "has a natural wonder. [It is] unparalleled throughout the rest of the world."

It also holds a key to Earth's past. Oceans can dry up. Deserts can vanish. But nature records what happens. The Grand Canyon's fossils and rocks tell the story of big changes from many years ago.

The Grand Canyon brings out the scientist in each of its visitors. They can hunt for fossils. They can see the many layers of rocks. The canyon is more than just awesome scenery. It is more than just a place for geologists to study. It is a place to explore and enjoy.

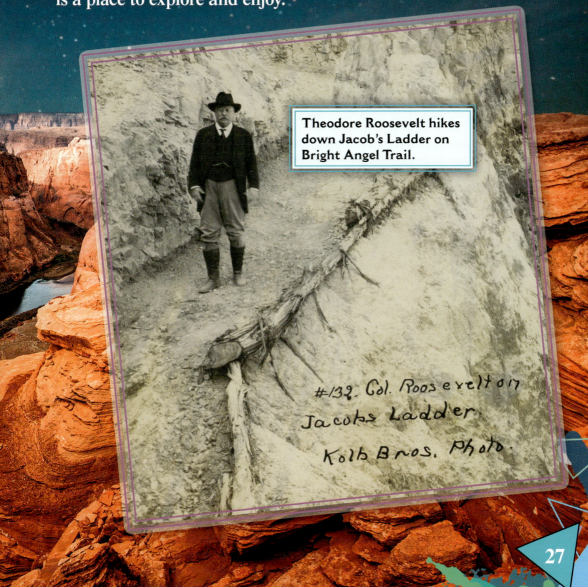

Theodore Roosevelt hikes down Jacob's Ladder on Bright Angel Trail.

Problem Solving

A new group of visitors is ready to saddle up and ride. Five mules, Arrow, Joo Joo, Lottie, Owl, and Pups, will lead them down the Bright Angel Trail. Once they get to the bottom of the Grand Canyon, everyone will rest. They will spend the night at the famous Phantom Ranch. The next morning, they will head back up the South Kaibab Trail on the same mules. Use the graph and table to answer the questions about the trip.

1. About how many total kilometers will the visitors ride?

2. About how many total kilometers will all five of the mules travel on this trip?

3. This trek adds one more round-trip to each mule's record. Make a new frequency table to show how many round-trips the mules have completed.

4. Use the new frequency table to answer the following questions:

    a. How many round-trips has Owl made?

    b. About how many total kilometers has Joo Joo traveled?

    c. How many more round-trips will Arrow have to make to have two times as many as Lottie?

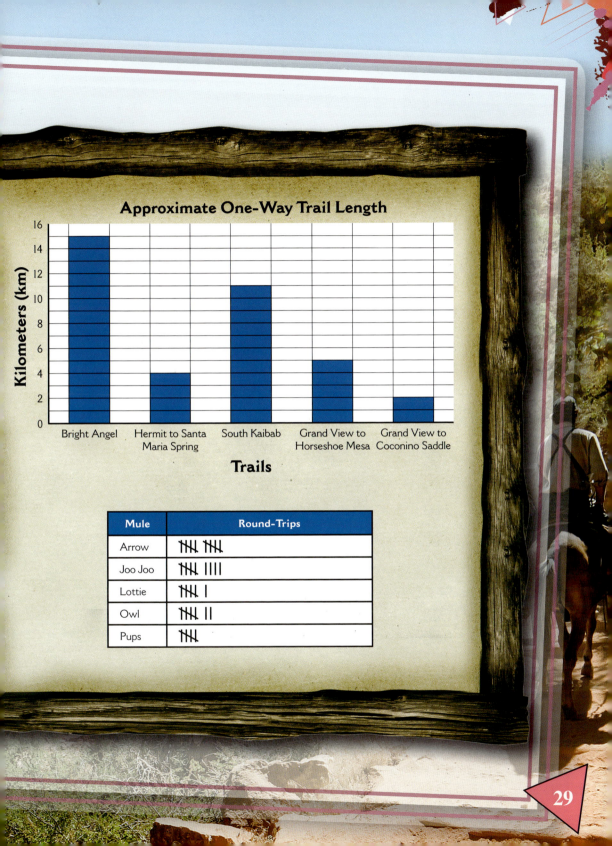

Glossary

cross-section—a view that shows what the inside of something looks like after it's been cut

decompose—to slowly break down

environment—the natural world

erosion—movement of weathered rock and sediment

fossil—dead plants and animals that have been preserved in rocks

geologists—scientists who study rocks and soil to learn about Earth's history

preserved—kept in its original state or in good condition

sediment—very small pieces of rock, such as sand, gravel, and dust

species—groups of animals or plants that are similar and can produce young animals or plants

wrangler—a person who takes care of horses, mules, or cattle

Index

brachiopods, 24–25

Bright Angel Trail, 8, 27–28

Colorado River, 4, 10, 13

crinoids, 24

cross-section, 14

Elves Chasm Gneiss 8

erosion, 13

fossil, 21–22, 24–27

geologists, 14, 18, 27

Grand Canyon Supergroup Rocks, 15

horn corals, 22

Jacob's Ladder, 27

Layered Paleozoic Rocks, 15

limestone, 18, 22, 24

mule, 4, 6–8, 28–29

Phantom Ranch, 28

Roosevelt, Theodore, 26–27

sandstone, 18, 21–22

sedimentary rocks, 18, 21

shale, 18, 21–22

South Kaibab Trail, 6, 8, 12, 28

Toroweap Point, 4

trilobites, 22–23

Vishnu Basement Rocks, 15

31

Answer Key

Let's Explore Math

page 5:
1. 2015
2. about 1,100,000 more visitors in 2015
3. about 500,000 more visitors in 2014
4. 200,000 visitors

page 7:
1. 5 more round-trips
2. 1 fewer round-trip
3. 37 round-trips total

page 9:
1. Bright Angel; about 30 km
2. Grand View to Horseshoe Mesa; the bar is higher
3. Grand View to Coconino Saddle and Hermit to Santa Maria Spring
4. 2 km

page 19:
1. Redwall Limestone
2. Muav Limestone and Bright Angel Shale
3. 200 ft.

page 25:
1. Crinoids; 12
2. Brachiopods and trilobites; 6 of each
3. Crinoids

Problem Solving

1. about 26 km
2. about 130 km
3. Frequency tables should show Arrow with 11 tally marks, Joo Joo with 10 tally marks, Lottie with 7 tally marks, Owl with 8 tally marks, and Pups with 6 tally marks.
4. a. 8 round-trips
   b. 260 km
   c. 3 more round-trips